Water and the Weather

Columbus, OH

SRAonline.com

 SRA

Send all inquiries to this address:
SRA/McGraw-Hill
4400 Easton Commons
Columbus, OH 43219

ISBN: 978-0-07-608668-9
MHID: 0-07-608668-2

2 3 4 5 6 7 8 9 NOR 13 12 11 10 09

The **McGraw·Hill** Companies

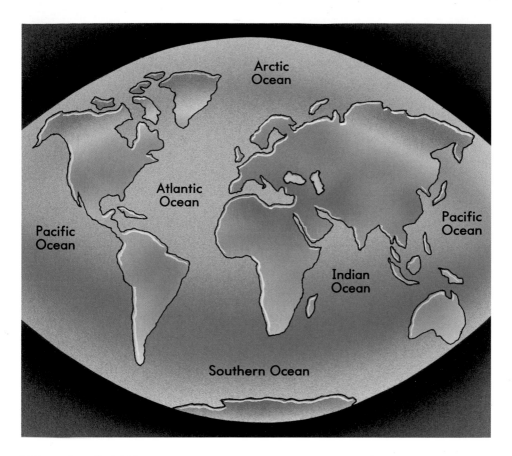

Wonderful Water

Water is important to life on Earth. Plants and animals depend on water to survive. Water can be found in many places on Earth. Oceans cover almost three-fourths of Earth's surface. They hold 97 percent of all water on Earth.

Earth's water may also be found in a river, lake, or reservoir. Water can be frozen in a glacier. It can be found underground. A small amount can even be found in the air.

Precipitation

Runoff

The Water Cycle and Weather

Water on Earth is always moving. The sun heats Earth's oceans unevenly. Some ocean water is hot. Some is cold. The difference in temperature makes currents in the oceans circulate. These currents heat or cool the air above the ocean. This makes the air circulate as well.

At the ocean's surface, tiny particles of water rise into the air. These particles are called water vapor. The process that makes water vapor is evaporation. As the air moves, it carries water vapor from place to place.

Condensation

Evaporation

    High in the sky, air is cooler. Cool air makes particles of water vapor come together. They form clouds. This process is called condensation. As a cloud grows, its load of water gets heavier. Eventually the water falls to Earth as rain, snow, or hail. Falling water is called precipitation.

    Some precipitation soaks into the ground. Some evaporates back into the air. Some becomes drinking water. But mostly it flows into streams and rivers. Over time, it will have flowed back to the ocean. Then the water cycle begins again.

Oceans and Weather

Weather is the pattern of wind, precipitation, and temperature in a place. Because the oceans help heat and cool the air, they greatly affect Earth's weather.

The equator gets the most sunlight on Earth. Here the ocean is warmest. Heat from the ocean is transferred to the air. So the air near the equator is warm too.

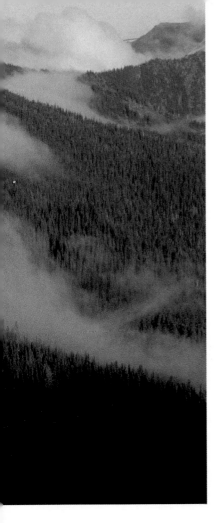

Near the North and South poles, Earth gets the least sunlight. These regions have the coldest ocean water. The air here is cold.

Air moves from areas of high pressure to areas of low pressure. As it moves, the air carries water vapor. This water vapor becomes precipitation.

Different places receive different amounts of precipitation. A desert receives little rain. A rain forest receives a lot.

Near mountains, rainfall varies. As clouds move over a mountain, precipitation becomes lighter. On one side of a mountain it may be raining. On the other side it may be completely dry.

Severe Storms

Warm ocean water and low air pressure can lead to a severe storm forming. This can happen in the Atlantic Ocean near the equator.

Eye

The wind in this kind of storm moves in a giant circle. At the center is a calm spot called the eye. This type of storm needs warm ocean water to survive. If the storm stays over warm water, its raging winds begin to blow harder. When the winds reach 74 miles per hour, this storm becomes a hurricane.

A hurricane may create a storm surge. In a storm surge the ocean rises. The waves can be 20 feet high when they reach a coastline.

Conditions must be just right for a hurricane to survive. For example, cool air and cool water will make the winds die down. Land will also cause a hurricane to lose its power. If a hurricane does not run into cool ocean water, it will pick up speed until it runs into land.

Useful Winds

The oceans also give us monsoons. A monsoon is a wind that changes direction as the seasons change. Monsoons blow from cold areas to warm areas.

In many places, the temperature changes with the seasons. The air gets cold in one season and hot in another. But over an ocean the temperature does not vary much.

Monsoons blow from cold areas to warm areas. So as seasons change on land, a monsoon's direction changes too.

A summer monsoon starts above the ocean and blows toward the land. It often brings rain. This is because the air has picked up water vapor from the ocean.

A winter monsoon is drier. Winter monsoons start above the cold land. They blow to the warmer ocean.

Many cultures depend on monsoons. For example, farmers use these patterns of rain to know when to plant their crops.

Rain from a monsoon

What Is El Niño?

Another weather condition is El Niño. It occurs in the Pacific Ocean. It is the unusual warming of the Pacific Ocean. It happens about every three to six years. Scientists are not sure why it happens.

They believe it has to do with trade winds. These are cool winds from high-pressure areas. Sometimes they do not blow as strongly as they normally do. Winds from high-pressure areas cool the ocean water. When they are not blowing as strongly, the ocean water warms to unusually high temperatures.

El Niño is linked to weather changes around the planet. For example, when the Pacific Ocean is unusually warm, more rain falls in parts of South America.

An El Niño wave

Warm ocean waters then move toward the poles. They cause harsh winter storms. Areas near the North and South poles might have more snow than usual. This is a result of El Niño.

Studying the Ocean

The National Oceanic and Atmospheric Administration (NOAA) is a program run by the United States government. Part of NOAA is the Climate Prediction Center (CPC).

The CPC studies the weather. It tries to predict when bad weather will occur. It tries to predict droughts, hurricanes, and bitterly cold winters. The CPC has become best known for studying El Niño. It predicts the effects this weather condition will have.

Predicting when and where bad weather may occur can help prevent problems. For example, the CPC claims to have saved people millions of dollars. It predicted that El Niño would cause heavy rains on the West Coast. People were ready for them.

The CPC studies weather patterns. It studies the ocean. In this way, the CPC can predict extreme weather months ahead of time. The CPC hopes to continue helping people prepare for bad weather.

Vocabulary

reservoir (re´ zə vwär´) (page 3) *n*. A lake, often artificial, for storing water.

glacier (glā´ shûr) (page 3) *n*. A huge mass of ice formed from unmelted snow, usually found in the polar regions or in high mountains.

circulate (sûr´ kyə lāt) (page 4) *v*. To flow around freely.

particles (pär´ ti kəlz) (page 4) *n*. Plural form of **particle:** A tiny piece.

flowed (flōd) (page 5) *v*. Past tense of **flow:** To move as water does.

transferred (trants fûrd´) (page 6) A form of the verb **transfer:** To pass along.

raging (rā´ jing) (page 9) *adj*. Violent; wild.

linked (linkt) (page 12) A form of the verb **link:** To connect.

Comprehension Focus: Asking Questions

1. After reading this book, write down two questions you have about how oceans affect the weather.

2. What are two new questions you have about hurricanes or monsoons? Where could you find the answers to these questions?